Armor of the Deutsches Afrikakorps

Text by Tom Cockle
Color plates by Arkadiusz Wróbel

ISBN 962-361-631-7
printed in Hong Kong

Acknowledgements
_All of the photographs published in this book are taken from
the Tank Museum Collection, Bovington, the Central Military
Archive, Warsaw and James V. Crow, Illinois._

INTRODUCTION

In early February 1941, the Italian Army was on the brink of a disastrous defeat in North Africa. The British Army had been steadily pushing them back from Egypt since 9 December 1940 and on 5 February had cut off their retreat along the coastal road at Beda Fomm. Within two days, their army lay shattered with only 7,000 weak and demoralized troops barring the way to a British advance into Tripolitania. The British had destroyed an Italian Army of four corps, capturing 130,000 prisoners, 400 tanks and about 1,300 guns against the loss of 500 killed, 1,373 wounded and 55 missing.

The situation in North Africa had not escaped the attention of Adolf Hitler. An Italian defeat could seriously undermine the Fascist regime and affect the Axis partnership. In October 1940, Generalmajor Wilhelm Ritter von Thoma had been sent to North Africa to investigate the possibilities of sending aid, but the matter had been dropped until the British attacks in December threatened to defeat the Italians. On 22 January 1941, the British captured the port of Tobruk and the Germans were reluctantly forced to act. Plans were made to send X Fliegerkorps to Sicily to attack the Royal Navy and British shipping in the Mediterranean and to send 5.leichte Division to North Africa in February. After the defeat at Beda Fomm, the plan was changed to a send a Panzer Korps by the addition of 15.Panzer-Division, to be sent as shipping allowed in March.

Hitler chose as the commander of the new Deutsches Afrika Korps, Generalleutnant Erwin Rommel, who had served as commander of the Führerbegleit Bataillon from 1938 to 1940 and with distinction as commander of 7.Panzer-Division in France in 1940. The DAK was to be under the command of Italian General Gariboldi but was to be employed as a single unit under Rommel. He had the right to appeal any order given by the Italian General, to the OKH in Berlin, if he thought it would jeopardize his command. After meeting with Mussolini and the Italian Commando Supremo in Rome on 11 February, Rommel and his staff flew to Tripoli next day.

On 14 February, the first German units started to arrive in Tripoli harbor. After a march past, the units were immediately sent east towards El Agheila where Rommel planned to establish a forward line of defense. Gariboldi disagreed, wanting a line farther west, but Rommel ignored this and sent each unit east as it arrived.

The DAK made its first contact with the British forces on 24 February, destroying three armored cars and one truck and capturing another armored car with no losses of their own. On 23 March, German reconnaissance reported that El Agheila was lightly held and Rommel ordered 5.leichte Division to capture the town next day. Quickly, this was followed up with an attack on Mersa Brega on 31 March. The British failed to take up the attack and withdrew, allowing the Germans to advance to Agedabia. By now, Rommel was unable to resist the temptation to pursue the retreating British. He sent a detachment of armored cars in pursuit along the coast road to Benghazi, which fell on 4 April, and a column of tanks and guns cross country towards Mechili, arriving there on 6 April. Some of the German units were running low on petrol, and Rommel, while personally delivering some to a stranded artillery column, narrowly avoided capture when he ran into an enemy force after losing his way. At this same time, the DAK captured British Generals O'Connor and Neame when their driver became lost and drove into the German lines. By 11 April the British had been completely thrown out of Cyrenaica, except for a small force surrounded in the port of Tobruk. An assault on the fortress by 5.leicht Division on 14 April and another on 30 April, were defeated soundly and the British settled in for a siege that was to last almost a year. The failure to take Tobruk would have far reaching effects on the DAK. It was the only suitable port for more than 1,000 miles between Tripoli and Alexandria and its capture would have shortened Rommel's supply lines considerably. In addition, its continued resistance provided a morale boosting effect to the Allies.

On 25 April, the Germans attacked Halfaya Pass and pushed the British back to Buq Buq on the coast. Rommel was ecstatic. In just over two weeks, he had captured back all the territory the British had taken from the Italians. The Germans began to consolidate their gains, building fortifications and laying mine fields and wire, at both Halfaya Pass and Sollum Pass.

Under pressure from Churchill to relieve Tobruk, General Wavell launched an attack against Halfaya Pass on 15 May, code named Operation 'Brevity'. The pass was quickly recaptured along with Fort Capuzzo after some heavy fighting. Rommel brought up reinforcements and retook Fort Capuzzo and then the pass on 27 May. The garrison at the pass was reinforced and placed under the command of Hauptmann Wilhelm Bach, who would later win fame defending it.

Despite their failure, the British were not discouraged. Having received replacements of tanks and men, Wavell again attacked Halfaya Pass on 15 June in Operation 'Battleaxe'. Rommel had been alerted by British radio activity of the impending attack and the German gunners were waiting. The dug in 88's knocked out eleven Matilda Mk. II's on the first day. In the meantime, the Germans had also received reinforcements. 15.Panzer-Division had arrived in three convoys on 24 April, 2 and 6 May. While 5.leichte Division moved against Sidi Omar, Pz.Rgt.8 of 15.Panzer-Division was involved in heavy fighting with 4th and 7th Armored Brigades at Fort Capuzzo. Now 5.leichte Division and 15.Panzer-Division were directed towards Halfaya Pass to try and trap the British forces, but they managed to escape to the east, leaving more than 220 of their tanks on the battlefield, 87 of which were completely destroyed. While the British claimed to have destroyed over 100 tanks, the Germans put their losses 25.

As a result, General Wavell was replaced by General Sir Claude Auchinleck. On the other hand, Rommel was promoted to General der Panzertruppe on 1 July and his command elevated to a Panzergruppe on 15 August. Another German division, Afrika Division z.b.V., was formed from various independent units already serving in North Africa plus additional troops brought in by air and assigned to Rommel's command. Panzergruppe Afrika consisted of the DAK with 5.leichte Division, 15.Panzer-Division, Afrika Division z.b.V. and the Italian 55 Savona Infantry Division plus the XXI Italian Corps with four infantry divisions, 17 Pavia, 25 Bologna, 27 Brescia and 102 Trento Motorized.

The first operation carried out by the new Panzergruppe Afrika, took place in September 1941, when they attacked what was mistakenly believed to be a huge

British fuel and supply dump at Bir Khireigat just inside the Egyptian border. No dump was found and Rommel turned his attention back to Tobruk.

The British continued to build up their strength, forming the new Eighth Army, with troops from Australia, New Zealand, India and South Africa, with General Sir Alan Cunningham as the new commander. Operation 'Crusader' was launched 18 November with the aim of cutting off the German garrison at Halfaya Pass and relieving Tobruk. When Rommel realized the extent of the British attack, he directed 21.Panzer-Division, newly reorganized from 5.leicht Division, to strike east to Sidi Azeiz and from there, to Gabr Saleh, where they engaged and inflicted heavy losses on 4th Armored Brigade. On 21 November, Rommel ordered DAK to attack towards Sidi Rezegh where 7th Armored Brigade had overrun the airfield destroying several aircraft on the ground. The battle raged on with both sides suffering heavy losses. British losses had convinced Rommel that he should send the DAK towards the frontier and cut off as much of Eighth Army as possible. With Rommel in the lead in his staff car, DAK sped eastwards along the Trigh el Abd, scattering many of the enemy before him. General Cunningham himself was almost captured when the plane he had just boarded was shelled while taking off. Meanwhile, Rommel had problems of his own when his car broke down. Fortunately, he was picked up by General Cruwell in his captured British Mammoth ACV. Having difficulty finding their way back through the wire along the frontier, they were forced to leaguer overnight, always fearful of being discovered by one of the many enemy patrols that passed close by.

Despite heavy losses to the British, German losses had also weakened DAK considerably. By early December, with few tanks in operating condition and supplies running low, Rommel came to the conclusion that he might have to withdraw from Cyrenaica. Only about one third of the supplies sent in the previous month had arrived and Rommel was told he could not expect reinforcements until January 1942. The British had lifted the siege of Tobruk on 26 November after 242 days. On 7/8 December, the withdrawal began. By 10 January, the Germans had safely retreated behind the Italian defensive line at El Agheila. The pursuing British, now short of supplies, halted as well.

On 5 January, the first reinforcements of any appreciable size arrived including 54 tanks, 20 armored cars, large numbers of anti-aircraft guns and artillery along with large quantities of fuel and ammunition. The majority of the new tanks were allotted to 15.Panzer-Division. Rommel renewed the offensive and on 21 January recaptured Agedabia and Beda Fomm. Intelligence reports indicated the British were having severe supply problems themselves and this action then quickly turned into a major assault. Taking Benghazi on 29 January, they continued to push the retreating Eighth Army back to the Gazala Line in the next few days. Low on supplies, Rommel halted his advance. On 30 January, Hitler elevated the status of Rommel's command to that of a Panzerarmee, and for the next few months there was a lull in the fighting while both sides built up their strength.

On 26 May, the Italian X & XXI Corps attacked the Gazala Line opposite the 1st South African Division to give the impression of a main thrust at Gazala while the entire German mobile force swept around the Free French held Bir Hacheim in the south and headed for the coast in the British rear. For two days, the Germans were held in battle in the area of Sidi Muftah, which came to be known as the 'Cauldron'. On 12 June, the panzers broke out to the south and east, beating off numerous British counter-attacks. The next day the British fell back from the Gazala Line to Tobruk and farther east and by 18 June, German forces had once again surrounded Tobruk. They began their attack on the morning of 20 June and the next day the garrison finally surrendered. This was the highlight of Rommel's career in North Africa and Hitler promoted him to Field Marshall, at the time the youngest in the German Army. Having lost more than 50,000 men and much of its armor, Eighth Army was given permission to withdraw to Mersa Matruh. Under continuous pressure from DAK, the British fell back to the more defensible El Alamein.

Rommel's attention now turned to Cairo. He had requested command of all the Italian troops in North Africa be turned over to him and permission to pursue the British to the Nile before they had a chance to recover. With Hitler's and Mussolini's approval, he began to plan the attack. As the DAK began to advance against Mersa Matruh on 26 June, Field Marshall Kesselring arrived at Rommel's headquarters to discuss the situation. He

had been opposed to Rommel's plan and argued against it, but Rommel was firm and unwavering. Mersa Matruh fell to the Germans on the morning of 29 June, by which time 21.Panzer-Division was close to Fuka, some 45 miles farther east. By the time his army reached the British lines at El Alamein, they were down to 55 tanks and had outrun their support. Ahead lay a 45 mile front stretching from the Mediterranean in the north to the impassable Qattara Depression in the south and the exhausted troops were being continually harassed by the Royal Air Force. After a number of unsuccessful attacks on 2-4 July, Rommel was forced to give it up. Limited British counter-attacks along the Ruweisat Ridge on 14 and 21 July convinced Rommel that a stalemate had been reached. Refusing to consider any further action until his forces were ready, Auchinleck was replaced by General Sir Harold Alexander and a new commander for Eighth Army brought in, Lieutenant-General Bernard Montgomery.

Rommel, in poor health, was totally absorbed during the month of August in planning the attack against the El Alamein positions and the advance to Alexandria. In fact, a number of German senior officers were suffering health problems brought on by poor diet and extreme conditions.

The attack began on 30 August with the main Axis assault group on the southern flank driving forward at night to position themselves south of the Alam Halfa Ridge on the morning of the 31st. They were held up by an unexpected mine field and then soft sand that caused the vehicles to use more fuel and delay their progress. As a result, they were unable to drive as far east as planned and were forced to turn north short of their goal and ran directly into the British defenses along the ridges. Surprise having been lost, it became impossible to break through to the coast. Under heavy air assault, Rommel was forced to concede defeat on 3 September and ordered a withdrawal. Between 30 August and 6 September, the Germans lost 2,910 men, 49 tanks, 55 guns and 395 other vehicles.

It was agreed that Rommel would be given a prolonged rest cure back in Germany and that a deputy, General Georg Stumme, would be sent to replace him during his absence. He arrived on 19 September to take up his new posting and on the 23rd, Rommel flew back to Germany.

When the British artillery opened up on the German positions on the evening of 23 October, it came as a complete surprise. With communications disrupted by the barrage, General Stumme personally headed for the front to evaluate the situation. Coming under shellfire, he apparently suffered a heart attack, although this was not known until the next day, and Generalleutnant von Thoma temporarily took over command. On the evening of 26 October, Rommel was back in North Africa. The situation he found was serious. The incessant artillery barrage was destroying his infantry and guns with some units down to half strength. 15.Panzer-Division had had their strength cut from 119 to 31 operational tanks. The Axis forces had entered the battle with 489 tanks, of which 278 were Italian M13s and M14s and only 30 were the Pz.Kpfw.IV Ausf.F2. The British fielded 1,029 tanks, of which 170 were Grants and 252 Shermans. Even though British losses amounted to about 300, many of which were repairable, they still had over 900 available on 26 October. On 1 November, Rommel was forced to withdraw his infantry in the north to prevent them from being encircled and two days later, Hitler issued one of his 'No Retreat' orders. The order was rescinded two days later when Rommel sent an aide to Hitler's headquarters to explain that if the order were followed, the Panzerarmee would be destroyed within days. By 9 November, the great retreat west had begun. Meanwhile, on the other side of the African continent, American troops had landed in French North Africa on 8 November.

What followed, from 4 November when the army retreated to Fuka, until the fall of Tripoli on 23 January 1943, was a long and expertly handled withdrawal. Fighting with determination, Panzerarmee Afrika fell back from one position to another, slowly followed by Eighth Army. Now under Italian command, they were ordered to hold the line at Mersa Brega. Rommel disagreed with this, wanting instead to withdraw all the way to Tunisia where the 12 mile wide Gabes Gap provided the best place to form a suitable defense. At a conference on 24 November with Kesselring and the Italian generals, Rommel stated that to hold the Mersa Brega line, he would need 50 new Mark IV Specials, the same number of the new 7.5cm PaK 40 anti-tank guns, 80 larger caliber guns, transporters, 4,000 tons of fuel and the same of ammunition plus Luftwaffe reinforcements. Instead, a few days later he

was ordered to attack with the forces available. Rommel issued an order for withdrawal and then flew to Rastenburg on 28 November to get Hitler's support. Instead, Rommel was promised supplies and told to hold the Mersa Brega positions. The Eighth Army arrived at these positions on 11 December. By this time, Rommel had realized if he held there, his forces would be encircled and so a few days previously had evacuated the position. When the British attack came on the 12th, the lines were empty, the Panzerarmee having withdrawn to Buerat.

By 19 January, they were moving back across the Tripolitanian border to Mareth, where a line of old French fortifications stood. Tripoli and its port were evacuated during the evening of 22 January, almost two years after the arrival of Rommel and first German troops. Rommel received a signal on 26 January that relieved him of his command once the Mareth Line had been reached, a decision that was later deferred.

After the unopposed American landings in North Africa, Kesselring began pouring reinforcements into Tunisia. By the end of November, there were some 25,000 German and Italian troops and 100 tanks including the new Tiger Is of s.Pz.Abt.501 and 10.Panzer-Division. They were under the command of General der Panzertruppe Walter Nehring, who had at one time commanded the DAK, until he had been wounded in August 1942. As the forces were built up, it was redesignated Pz.-A.O.K. 5 and on 9 December, Nehring handed over command to Generaloberst Jurgen von Arnim.

Both von Arnim's and Rommel's forces launched attacks in the direction of Kasserine Pass. Von Arnim's 10. and 21.Panzer-Divisions (21.Panzer was transferred to Pz.-A.O.K. 5 when it crossed the border into Tunisia) attacked through the Faid Pass to Sidi bou Zid on 14 February, winning a great victory against the inexperienced American troops. Rommel and his DAK attacked two days later through Gafsa, capturing the town without a fight. Rommel now saw an opportunity to thrust forward towards Tebessa and beyond, but von Arnim, suspicious of Rommel's motives, would not co-operate and sent his forces on a more limited advance towards Sbeitla. Rommel took Kasserine, inflicting heavy casualties on the American troops, on 18 February.

General Alexander, who took over control of the Allied forces, ordered no more withdrawals and reinforced the Allied positions at Thala and Sbiba, preventing an Axis breakthrough. On 22 February, Rommel called off the attacks and by 25 February, Kasserine was back in Allied hands. In terms of casualties, it was an Axis victory with some 10,000 Allied casualties against 2,000 Axis casualties. However, the Allies could afford to replace theirs.

Next Rommel attacked Eighth Army at Medenine on the Mareth Line on 6-7 March, where they lost 50 tanks, about one third of their strength, and were forced to pull back having achieved nothing. This would be Rommel's last battle in North Africa. He handed over his command to von Arnim and flew to Germany to beg Hitler, unsuccessfully, to save his army. Rommel expected to return, however Hitler refused to allow him to leave Germany.

On 20 March, Montgomery attacked the Mareth Line. A flanking assault to the south turned the German lines at El Hamma on 26 March, a success that he reinforced with an armored division and air support. To avoid being encircled, the Axis forces retired to Wadi Akarit.

By the middle of April, all the Axis forces had been squeezed into a small area around Tunis and Bizerte. They were heavily outnumbered in tanks and guns, the Allies fielding some 1,200 tanks and 500 guns to the 130 tanks and 500 guns of the Axis forces. The end was inevitable and on 12 May 1943, Generaloberst von Arnim surrendered.

The German Army in North Africa achieved a reputation that was second to none. Inspired by Rommel's dynamic leadership, the DAK in a short space of time, acquired a fearsome image that helped it win victories over a numerically superior enemy, with a bearing, skill and chivalry that was unmatched in any other theater of war. Masters of improvisation, they maintained an edge in technique and equipment over the Allies, much of which was adopted and used by them to the end of the war.

An Sd.Kfz.251/1 Ausf.B is unloaded from a transport ship in Tripoli in late February or early March 1941. It is one of the half-tracks of either 2.M.G.Bataillon or 8.M.G.Bataillon which arrived before Pz.Rgt.5. Note the unusually large swastika painted on the engine compartment for air recognition.

A Pz.Kpfw.III Ausf.G parades through Tripoli on March 12, 1941. Pz.Rgt.5 was originally formed as part of 3.Panzer-Division and had been in preparation for shipment to North Africa since October 1940, arriving in early March 1941. On February 5, 1941, Pz.Rgt.5 was officially transferred to the newly formed 5.leichte Division. During embarkation at Naples, 10 Pz.Kpfw.III and 3 Pz.Kpfw.IV were destroyed in a fire aboard ship. All of the vehicles still retained their dark gray (RAL 7021) paint schemes and displayed large, white outline tactical numbers.

After the parade, II.Abteilung left Tripoli heading east towards Sirte, arriving 4 days later after a series of night marches to avoid detection. The crew of this Pz.Kpfw.IV Ausf.D still wear their black Panzer uniforms which would soon be replaced by new tropical issue.

Two more Pz.Kpfw.IV Ausf.D of 8.Kompanie/Pz.Rgt.5 make their way through the desert in the days following their arrival. The dark gray paint is heavily covered with dust but this was not very effective camouflage in the desert environment.

Two Pz.Kpfw.IV Ausf.D followed by two Pz.Kpfw.II Ausf.A-C advance through the Arco dei Felini, located along the 'Via Balbia' on the Cyrenaica/Tripolitania border west of El Agheila. The large, white outline tactical numbers identify these vehicles as belonging to Pz.Rgt.5. Temperatures in the desert could be quite cold in the winter and spring, as is evidenced by the commander of the nearest Pz.Kpfw.II who is wearing his officers standard pattern European greatcoat.

An early production leichte Panzerspähwagen Sd.Kfz.222, armed with a 2cm KwK30 and a coaxial 7.92mm MG34, is followed by an Sd.Kfz.221 which was armed only with an MG34. The Sd.Kfz.222 shows a well worn paint scheme of desert sand paint applied over the dark gray base. No markings are visible on either vehicle.

A column of light transport vehicles is led by an early production schwere Panzerspähwagen Sd.Kfz.231 eight wheeled armored car fitted with the additional 8mm armored shield which was added to the front beginning in early 1940. The Horch Kfz.15 on the right displays a DAK palm emblem on the left mudguard and an unidentifiable tactical marking on the right on a patch of the original dark gray paint.

On April 14, 1941, Pz.Rgt.5 launched its first unsuccessful assault against Tobruk, losing several tanks during the attack to dug in British 25pdr. guns. The white outline tactical number '821' is barely visible on the turret of this knocked out Pz.Kpfw.IV Ausf.E, which has been fitted with additional 20mm side plates and 30mm front plates called 'Zusatzpanzer'. An internal explosion has blown off the driver's visor and 'Zusatzpanzer' and caused a fire that has burnt the rubber off some of the roadwheels.

A Pz.Kpfw.IV Ausf.D of Pz.Rgt.5, also destroyed during this battle, has the white outline tactical number '811' painted on the turret. These tanks had a hastily applied coat of sand yellow paint applied over the dark gray base as can be seen by the dark lines on the rear plate where the paint was applied with the tow cable still in place. A DAK palm emblem and white outline cross are the only other visible markings.

This Pz.Kpfw.IV Ausf.F1 has a white outline tactical number on the turret. Judging by the different style of numbers to those of 8.Kompanie vehicles, it is probably '403' from the 4.Kompanie of I.Abteilung. A black cross with a white outline has been painted on the side of the hull as well as on the smoke candle armored housing. The reversed swastika has obviously been added by the British after the battle. At the end of March 1941, Pz.Rgt.5 had 17 Pz.Kpfw.IV available.

A Pz.Kpfw.IV Ausf.E of Pz.Rgt.5 completely destroyed by an internal ammunition explosion that has blown off its turret. The 20mm and 30mm additional armor plates are quite visible in this photo. During the attack on Tobruk, 8.Kompanie lost 5 of its Pz.Kpfw.IV. Sand yellow paint has been applied in a thin, wavy pattern over the dark gray base. The object in front of the driver's visor is one of the return roller mounts from the side of the vehicle. This vehicle is still fitted with the early 36cm track.

A Pz.Kpfw.III Ausf.H of Pz.Rgt.5 captured at Tobruk being dismantled for evaluation by British troops. It is finished with sand yellow paint applied over the dark gray base and has a faint white outline tactical number 'II02' painted on the turret indicating it to be the command vehicle assigned to the II.Abteilung Adjutant. A small black DAK palm emblem was painted beside the ball mount MG on the front plate. The additional 30mm armor plate bolted on the front of the Ausf.H was impenetrable to the British 2pdr. tank and anti-tank guns in use at the time.

Another vehicle captured at Tobruk by the British was this Pz.Kpfw.II Ausf.A-C of Pz.Rgt.5 with the white outline tactical identification 'RA'. It was the vehicle assigned to the Regimental Arzt, or Medical Officer. Another photograph of this vehicle shows a stylized white caduceus painted behind the tactical identification. Other markings include a white outline national cross and white DAK palm emblems on the side and front. A small white letter 'G' can also be seen next to the DAK palm on the front. Here, the vehicle has been dug in as a static defense weapon by its new owners. Note the 15mm additional armor plates bolted to the mantlet.

A British soldier examines a gas mask beside a Pz.Kpfw.I Ausf.A of Pz.Rgt.5 that has been damaged by a mine. A white outline tactical number 'II25' is painted on the turret showing this to be a I.Abteilung staff vehicle. Other markings include a white DAK palm emblem on the front and sides of the hull. It has been camouflaged with a light coat of sand yellow applied over the dark gray base.

A Horch Kfz.15 carries a group of jubilant civilians along a street in Benghazi, April 18,1941. By this time, most vehicles had received a coat of sand yellow camouflage paint over their original dark gray color. The Horch carries the DAK palm emblem on its left mudguard and a white letter 'S' in a white outline circle on its right, both on a patch of the dark gray base. Barely visible behind the left headlight, is a yellow pennant with a black cross and a small black '4' in the upper left corner, indicating this is a staff vehicle of a Nachrichtung, or signals, Abteilung. There is also a small red pennant with a black swastika in a white circle behind the right headlight. Following behind is an Sd.Kfz.263 Panzerfunkwagen eight wheeled heavy armored radio car.

An 8.8cm FlaK18 raises a cloud of dust after firing at British targets in the Marsa el Brega area in April 1941. The gun has been painted with a light coat of sand yellow paint over the dark gray base and a small DAK palm emblem can be seen on a dark gray patch on the gun shield. There are 8 kill rings painted on the gun barrel which, at this early stage of German involvement in North Africa, were likely the result of earlier combat in Europe.

A Mercedes 170VK staff car on the outskirts of Benghazi in April 1941. It has been painted sand yellow over the dark gray base and has a white DAK palm emblem painted in white on a patch of the original dark gray. In the background is a Ford 3 ton lorrie which has been fitted with a dark green canvas cover.

Another Pz.Kpfw.II Ausf.A-C, this one without the additional 15mm plates bolted to the mantlet. The barrel of the 2cm KwK30 has been covered with a canvas sheath to protect it from sand and dirt.

A Pz.Kpfw.III Ausf.H rolls past an abandoned British Bofors 40mm anti-aircraft gun. Originally manufactured in Sweden in 1930, the Bofors 40mm gun was the most widely used anti-aircraft gun used during WWII and was still in service and production in 1974.

A knocked out early Pz.Kpfw.III Ausf.G of Pz.Rgt.5 with a white outline tactical number 'R03' identifying it as belonging to the Regimental Signals Officer. It has been painted with a light coat of sand yellow paint over the dark gray base and displays the DAK palm emblem on the front plate. The vehicle to the left is a British Daimler scout car.

The crew of this Pz.Bef.Wg.III Ausf.H pose with their war booty - some captured bottles of wine. The turret was bolted in place and the large frame antenna on the engine deck distinguished this tank from the standard gun tank. Later in the war, it was replaced by the less conspicuous star antenna. Two crew members wear the tropical sun helmet which, though unpopular, continued to be worn until the end of the campaign.

Another Pz.Bef.Wg.III Ausf.H. It was equipped with a dummy 3.7cm gun with a ball mounted MG34 next to it in the mantlet and had additional 30mm armor plates bolted to the front. A pistol port replaced the hull mounted MG34. The vehicle has been painted with a light coat of sand yellow over the dark gray base, a patch of which surrounds the DAK palm emblem on the front plate. Next to the pistol port, a white letter 'G' can be seen, probably indicating this vehicle also belongs to Pz.Rgt.5.

13

This Pz.Bef.Wg.III Ausf.H has been knocked out somewhere along the Mediterranean coast. The only visible marking is the white outline national cross on the side of the hull and a dummy 5cm gun replaces the earlier dummy 3.7cm gun. A spacer ring has been bolted to the early drive sprocket to accommodate the newer 40cm track.

The crews of two schwerer Panzerspähwagen (Fu) Sd.Kfz.232 and an Sd.Kfz.231 armored car form a leaguer in the desert, digging protective hole and filling sandbags. Rocks and sandbags are piled up around the wheels of the vehicles to protect them from shell splinters or strafing aircraft. Anoth photo of the armored car closest to the camera clearly shows the camouflage coat is dried mud.

An 8.8cm FlaK18 in full recoil. In an emergency, the gun could fired while still limbered but the greatest accuracy was achieved wh properly emplaced. It was as an anti-tank weapon that the '88' fi gained notoriety in North Africa.

14

Generalleutnant Erwin Rommel and some of his staff officers near Tobruk in May 1941. The attack to take the town had failed and his attention would now be directed towards the British forces to the east.

A totally destroyed Pz.Kpfw.III Ausf.G of Pz.Rgt.8. A red with white outline tactical number '1' can be seen on the side of the turret along with a small red '114' in the manner common to vehicles of this regiment. Pz.Rgt.8 arrived in Tripoli in three convoys, the first of which included 1.Kompanie and arrived on April 25, 1941. This vehicle was blown up by the British after its capture.

An internal explosion has blown out the front plate of this Pz.Kpfw.II Ausf.A. The red 'Wolfsangel' symbol of Pz.Rgt.8 is visible on the front of the stowage bin located on the right mudguard. Behind it, a black national cross with a white outline can be seen. Pz.Rgt.8 was equipped with 45 Pz.Kpfw.II when it shipped to North Africa in April, 1941.

15

Unusual brothers-in-arms. Here a Pz.Kpfw.IV Ausf.D stands beside a captured Matilda Mk.2. While the Matilda lacked firepower - it was equipped with a 2pdr. gun (40mm), its German opponent's flaw was its poor armor protection (30mm at the nose). Pz.Rgt.8 of 15.Panzer-Division captured 7 Matilda's from the British at Halfaya Pass on May 27, 1941. These captured vehicles were prominently marked with oversized black and white outline national crosses so that German gunners would recognize them.

German troops occupy an abandoned British position somewhere east of Tobruk in June 1941. Smoke from burning vehicles rises in the distance behind two Pz.Kpfw.II Ausf.A-C.

Men from one the Division Nachrichtung Abteilungen wait t arrival of a Feis Storch at a dese airstrip. Pictured he in the foreground is Pz.Bef.Wg.III Ausf along with Panzerfunkwagen Sd.Kfz.263 and Sd.Kfz.251/1 Ausf that has had a custo made frame anten fabricated by the fie workshop attached increase the range its radios.

Three Horch Kfz.15 personnel cars and an Sd.Kfz.10 travel across the open desert near Tobruk in August 1941. Two of the vehicles are towing 2cm laK30 anti-aircraft guns and the half-track is towing a 7.5cm leIG 18. The Horch nearest the camera is carrying a divisional command pennant with a black ver white over red band.

An early Pz.Kpfw.III Ausf.G of Pz.Rgt.5 raises a cloud of dust as it avels down a desert road. The additional roadwheels and spare track also erved to provide additional protection for the vehicle. It has been painted ith a light coat of sand yellow applied over the dark gray base color. The oject visible to the left of the turret is a telegraph pole.

This Pz.Kpfw.III Ausf.H is identified by the additional 30mm armor plates bolted on the front of the hull and welded to the front of the superstructure. The crew has added several sets of extra spare track links to further increase the protection.

The crew of a Pz.Kpfw.III Ausf.H or early Ausf.J of Pz.Rgt.8 take a break from the fighting. Part of the original tactical number can still be seen on the side of the turret, probably '534', along with a new number '5', indicating the company number, painted in red in front. Just to the left of it can be seen the Divisional emblem, a red triangle with a vertical line through it.

One of the three AEC Armored Command Vehicles captured from the British at Mechili in April, 1941, two of which were retained by Rommel for his personal use. One was named 'Max' and the other, Rommel's favorite, named 'Moritz', which has been painted in white. It appears to have the new German markings added over the original British disruptive camouflage paint scheme. These include an oversized black with white outline national cross on the front, a black and white command flag for a Panzer Group Commander with a black DAK palm emblem over it and a black tactical sign for a headquarters vehicle. A German vehicle registration number has also been painted on.

The remains of three Pz.Kpfw.III and a lorry from Pz.Rgt.8 burn in the background after an intense battle. The Pz.Kpfw.III on the right is an Ausf.H while the one beyond it is an Ausf.G. In the foreground is a kl.Pz.Bef.Wg.I Ausf.B that has had its rear engine deck blown off. Part of the tactical number, probably a black 'R', can be seen on the open hatch door.

A close up photo of the Pz.Kpfw.III Ausf.H clearly shows the additional 30mm plates bolted to the hull and welded to the superstructure.

Two photos of a kl.Pz.Bef.Wg.I Ausf.B of Pz.Rgt.5 captured by the British after 'Operation Crusader'. A British Evaluation Report stated the color was light green but it is more likely that it was sand yellow that may have appeared light green when applied over the dark gray base. Visible markings include a thin white outline tactical number 'I03' indicating this to be the vehicle assigned to the I.Abteilung Signals Officer. A white DAK palm emblem is painted on the rear angled plate of the superstructure and the original divisional emblem of 3.Panzer-Division, an inverted 'Y' with two short vertical bars to the right of it, is visible below the tactical number, probably in yellow. These two markings were repeated on the front of the hull as well. On October 1, 1941, 5.leichte Division was reformed to 21.Panzer-Division and its new divisional emblem, a white 'D' with a horizontal line through it has also been painted on the front. This vehicle is currently on display at the RAC Tank Museum at Bovington.

A Pz.Kpfw.III Ausf.G from Pz.Rgt.5 totally destroyed and consumed by fire during 'Operation Crusader' south-east of Tobruk. When the British attack began on November 18, 1941, Pz.Rgt.5 reported a strength of 35 Pz.Kpfw.II, 68 Pz.Kpfw.III, 17 Pz.Kpfw.IV and 4 Pz.Bef.Wg.III. On November 22, their strength was down to 18 Pz.Kpfw.II, 32 Pz.Kpfw.III and 7 Pz.Kpfw.IV.

A Pz.Kpfw.IV Ausf.F1 of 4.Kompanie/Pz.Rgt.8 probably abandoned for lack of fuel during 'Operation Crusader' in November 1941. Several photos show at least three Pz.Kpfw.IV of 4.Kompanie close together with no apparent battle damage. Vehicles of this regiment are characterized by their single digit tactical numbers indicating the company to which they belonged.

Two photos of a Pz.Kpfw.IV Ausf.D of 4.Kompanie/Pz.Rgt.8 after 'Operation Crusader'. The crew has made an attempt to increase the armor protection of their vehicle by placing additional spare track links in front of the hull and turret. In the second photo, a burning object has been placed on the engine deck causing a great deal of smoke but not much fire, which may indicate this was staged for propaganda purposes. On November 23, 1941, Pz.Rgt. lost 9 of the 16 Pz.Kpfw.IV available at the start of the day.

A dead crewman lies next to this Pz.Kpfw.IV Ausf.D from .Kompanie/Pz.Rgt.5 in the aftermath of 'Operation Crusader', while a seemingly unconcerned group of British soldiers examine the vehicle. A white outline tactical number '414' is painted on the sides of the turret and rear stowage in. A white DAK palm emblem can e seen on the front and left side long with a white outlined black ational cross on each side. It was et on fire later, probably to prevent from being recovered by the Germans.

A Pz.Kpfw.III Ausf.G of .Kompanie/Pz.Rgt.8, captured by the British and photographed on ecember 20, 1941. It has been efitted with the new 40cm wide acks and redesigned drive procket along with a couple of the ider roadwheels. Curiously, the ennant the British officer is olding has the inscription '1 komp' script beside the skull. The emains of three Pz.Kpfw.IV can be een in the background.

British soldiers gather around a schwere Panzerspähwagen (Fu Sd.Kfz.232 while an officer likely addresses them on vehicle recognition Other than the vehicle registration number, the only other markings are the white outline black national cross on the side of the hull.

A schwere Panzerspähwagen Sd.Kfz.231 loaded o a British transpor truck for removal to vehicle dump possibly for furthe evaluation. The san yellow camouflag paint is well wor showing the dark gra base underneath Markings are limited t the vehicle registratio number plate and th original white outlin national cross.

Two 8.8cm FlaK 18 anti-aircraft guns limbered up behind their Sd.Kfz.7 half-tracked towing vehicles. There are no markings evident, but they probably belong to one of the independent Flak-Regiments that served in North Africa. The photo was taken in December 1941.

An Sd.Kfz.7 half-track towing a 15cm sFH 18 howitzer into a prepared emplacement in January 1942. The sand yellow camouflage paint is almost worn off the half-track exposing the dark gray base while the gun shows wear mostly around the gun barrel. A small enclosure has been set up using some wooden crates and the wicker shipping containers that the 15cm projectiles were shipped in. The tactical sign for a towed artillery company can be seen on the left mudguard of the Sd.Kfz.7.

A column of armored and softskin vehicles from 5.Panzer-Division drive east in February 1942. Pz.Kpfw.III from Pz.Rgt.8 take the lead followed up by a transport truck and an Sd.Kfz.10 half-track towing an ammunition trailer. A white outline tactical sign for a Panzer Division appears on the rear of the half-track and is repeated on the rear of the trailer as well. Also visible are the white DAK palm emblem and the red 'Wolfsangel' emblem of Pz.Rgt.8. Two stone cairns have been erected beside the road to mark the way.

An Sd.Kfz.11 half-track towing a 10.5cm leFH 18 howitzer along the 'Via Balbia' in February, 1942, with the city of Derna and the Mediterranean visible in the background. Except for the vehicle registration plate and a tactical sign for a towed artillery company on its left mudguard, there are no markings. The vehicle and gun appear to be in their original dark gray paint scheme and may have just recently arrived in North Africa.

A Pz.Kpfw.II Ausf.F stands guard in the desert while a vehicle burns in the distance, February 1942. The edge of a stenciled on tactical number, either a '3' or an '8' painted in black, is visible on the side of the turret. Virtually all of the sand yellow camouflage paint has been worn away leaving the vehicle in its original dark gray color.

A British Humber Mk.II armored car which has been captured and incorporated into one of the Panzer Divisions in March 1942. It was common for the Germans to put to use any serviceable vehicles abandoned by the enemy, a practice not adopted by the British.

The sense of urgency is apparent on the faces of this Luftwaffe 8.8cm FlaK 36 gun crew as they rush to pick ammunition for their gun. Ammunition was stored in lockers on either side at the rear of the Sd.Kfz.7 half-tracked prime mover for easy access by the gun crew. A white DAK palm emblem has been painted on the mudguard of the Sd.Ah.202 gun carriage visible between the legs of the two crewmen.

Vehicles of the DAK stream across the desert in pursuit of the British forces near Acroma in June 1942. In the background are two Pz.Kpfw.III along with various staff cars, Kübelwagens and motorcycle combinations. The Sd.Kfz.253 in the middle of the picture is from t.Rgt.155, 21.Panzer-Division and is the subject of a color plate in the Concord book 'Wehrmacht Support Vehicles'.

Another British Humber Mk.II armored car and a 3-ton CMP-FAT-2 (Canadian Military Pattern - Field Artillery Tractor), commonly known as the Qua gun tractor, along with another unidentifiable vehicle. The armored car has been marked with oversize national crosses to plainly identify it to nervou German gunners, one of the hazards of using captured enemy equipment. The camouflage pattern on the gun tractor is not a standard British pattern an has probably been modified in the field with paint or mud.

A knocked out leichte gepanzerte Beobachtungskraftwagen Sd.Kfz.253 marked with a white DAK palm emblem and the tactical sign of the 1st company of a towed artillery unit painted on the front plate. Initially, these vehicles were assigned to Sturmartillerie units though apparently some found their way into normal artillery battalions. An internal fire has burned the paint off the side and caused the vehicle to settle as the heat destroyed the torsion bar suspension.

This Pz.Kpfw.III Ausf.J of 2.Kompanie/Pz.Rgt.8 was destroye near Tobruk in June 1942. The tactical number '2' is painted in red wi a white outline on each side of the turret. The national cross is blac with a white outline. While the Pz.Kpfw.III Ausf.J was more than capab when dealing with the Crusader and Stuart tanks, it was less power than the newly introduced Grant.

A Pz.Kpfw.III Ausf.G of 6.Kompanie/Pz.Rgt.5 rolls past the wrecks of British armor after the fall of Tobruk in June 1942. The tank on the right is a Cruiser Mk IVA of 2nd Armored Division while the vehicle on the left is a Marmon-Harrington Mk.II armored car. The Germans took 33,000 prisoners, captured over ,000 vehicles, thousands of tons of ammunition, 5,000 tons of food and 2,000 tons of precious fuel.

Two Pz.Kpfw.II Ausf.A-C from 8.Kompanie/Pz.Rgt.8. Other photos of these vehicles show that, in addition to the new black tactical number with a white outline, there is a white DAK palm emblem and red 15.Panzer-Division sign on the side of the turret.

British POWs fill their water canteens from a steel drum in June 1942. The Kübelwagen in the foreground is equipped with the large balloon sand tires and displays a very worn paint scheme. The stencil on the mudguard - 690-200-0.6atu - gives the tire and rim size in millimeters and the tire pressure in atmospheres.

27

The crew of this 8.8cm FlaK 18 rest in their foxholes during a lull in the fighting. The gun is still limbered on its trailer to allow it to be easily moved to a different location. After firing, the muzzle blast raised a large cloud of dust that permitted the enemy to quickly spot their location and bring in suppressing artillery fire.

Soldiers in a Horch Type 40 Kfz.15 staff car, followed by a Pz.Kpfw.III Ausf.H, smile for the camera as they pass by another car from the Propaganda Kompanie. The Horch is painted with sand yellow camouflage over the dark gray base which is starting to show through. The only visible marking is a small '94' painted on the right mudguard, a remnant of the vehicles original registration number.

The crew of this 15cm sFH 18 howitzer struggle to push the barrel back into its traveling position. This helped to distribute the weight more evenly between the gun carriage and the limber and made turning corners in built up areas easier, though this was seldom a problem encountered in North Africa.

The commander of this Pz.Bef.Wg.III Ausf.H intently scans the horizon with his binoculars. In the foreground is Rommel's early Sd.Kfz.250/5 half-track, nicknamed 'GREIF', which is painted on the left side in red with a white outline and on the right side in white outline only. Just visible behind the tank is a radio operator seated at a field radio. The turret of the Pz.Bef.Wg.III was fixed in place thus permitting the engine deck to be used for stowage of additional gear. This photo was taken on July 16, 1942.

This Pz.Kpfw.II Ausf.A-C has sustained mine damage to its track and running gear. It has been fitted with the later commander's cupola but lacks the additional 15mm armor plates bolted on to the mantlet. Most of the sand yellow camouflage paint is worn off by wind blown sand revealing the dark gray paint underneath.

Two Pz.Kpfw.III pass an Sd.Kfz.7 towing a 15cm sFH 18 howitzer heading in the opposite direction. The remains of a past battle, a truck chass[i]s stripped of any useful parts, lies in the foreground, a prophecy of things to come.

The driver of this Sd.Kfz.7 half-track negotiates his way over a small bridge across an anti-tank ditch that has been made up of large rocks and old fuel drums. A white DAK palm emblem has been painted on the side of the vehicle just behind the driver and a white air recognition band painted on top of the engine cover.

The driver of this BMW R-12 motorcycle combination[s] barters with the local inhabitants. The sand yello[w] camouflage paint has begun to wear off in some plac[es] leaving the dark gray paint underneath exposed. T[he] registration number on the front mudguard has be[en] removed by the censor.

This smiling crew member of a schwere Panzerfunkwagen Sd.Kfz.263 displays he fresh vegetables and fruit he has probably just bartered for including a cap full f eggs. The vehicle is finished in a patchy coat of sand yellow over the dark gray ase color. There is a black national cross with a white outline painted on the side f the hull. The telescoping mast antenna can be seen here partially raised.

Oberst Hans Cramer in the turret of his Pz.Bef.Wg.III Ausf.H, converses with another officer in a Horch Type 40 staff car bearing the command flag for an Army Corps Commander. As commander of Pz.Rgt.8 of 15.Panzer-Division, he was awarded the Knight's Cross for his part in capturing Sidi Aziz on May 16, 1941 and then Fort Capuzzo and Halfaya Pass. After being wounded, he served as Chief of Staff for the General Mobile Forces until he was promoted to Generalmajor and appointed commander of the unit. On March 1, 1943, he was given command of the DAK and promoted to General der Panzertruppe on May 1. His last act as commander was to sign the surrender documents on May 12, 1943.

This Pz.Kpfw.III Ausf.J loaded onto a 22/23 ton tank transporter trailer, Sd.Ah.116, has been captured by the British near Sidi Barani. A white tactical number 'I' indicates this is a I.Abteilung staff vehicle. White lines have also been painted around the edges of the rear stowage bin, probably to help identify it as a staff vehicle from the rear at long distances.

A burned out Pz.Kpfw.III Ausf.H of Pz.Rgt.5. A white DAK palm emblem and the divisional sign for 21.Panzer-Division can be seen on the front plate.

A Pz.Kpfw.III Ausf.H followed by a Pz.Kpfw.III Ausf.F - a vehicle rarely seen in the North African theater. A red tactical number '1' can be seen on the turret of the Ausf.H indicating it is from 1.Kompanie/Pz.Rgt.8. Several jerry cans are stowed in a specially built rack on the mudguard. There also seems to be another special rack on the rear of the engine deck storing some long wooden poles.

z.Kpfw.IV Ausf.D, Pz.Rgt.5, 5.leichte Division, Tripoli, March/April 1941

II./Pz.Rgt.5 arrived in Tripoli, Libya on March 8, 1941. Originally formed as one of the two Panzer-Regiments of 3.Panzer-Division, these vehicles were finished in their European dark gray (RAL 7021) paint scheme and had large, white outline tactical numbers painted on the sides of the turret and back of the turret stowage bin. The tactical number was repeated on a small, black rhomboid metal plate attached to each side and the rear of the vehicle. The divisional emblem of 3.Panzer-Division, an inverted 'Y' with two small vertical bars, was painted in yellow on the center of the front plate and just above and to the left of the rear towing pintle.

z.Bef.Wg.I Ausf.B, Pz.Rgt.5, 21.Panzer-Division, Libya, late 1941

This command version of the Pz.Kpfw.I has been finished with a light green paint applied over the dark gray (RAL 7021) base according to British Evaluation Report conducted after its capture. It is more likely that the color is sand yellow that appeared to the observer as a light green at the time. The tactical number 'I03' painted in white outline indicates this is the vehicle assigned to the 1.Abteilung Signals Officer. A small white DAK palm emblem is also painted on each side of the superstructure and on the top of the left rear plate. The tactical emblem of the division, a white 'D' with a horizontal line through it, appears on the front as well as on the rear plate below the smoke candle rack along with a solid white narrow style national cross. The 3.Panzer-Division tactical emblem is also faintly visible on the sides and front of the crew compartment, probably in its original yellow.

Pz.Kpfw.III Ausf.G, Pz.Rgt.5, 5.leichte Division, Soluch, April 1941

This Pz.Kpfw.III Ausf.G was assigned to the Regimental Signals Officer. It has been painted with a patchy coat of sand yellow (RAL 8000) over the dark gray (RAL 7021) base and features large, white tactical numbers on each side of the turret and on the rear stowage bin, in this case 'R03', which were typical for this unit. A DAK palm was painted in white in the center of the front plate.

Pz.Kpfw.II Ausf.B, Pz.Rgt.5, 5.leichte Division, Tobruk, April 1941

This is the command vehicle assigned to the Regimental Arzt or Medical Officer. It is finished with a patchy coat of sand yellow (RAL 8000) applied over the dark gray (RAL 7021) base. The tactical number 'RA' has been painted in white outline on the side of the turret along with stylized caduceus to the right of it. There is a white outline national cross on the left side of the hull with a dark gray center. A white DAK palm emblem is painted on each side and is also repeated on the front beside the driver's visor. A very faint white letter 'G' is also visible just to the right of the DAK palm on the front.

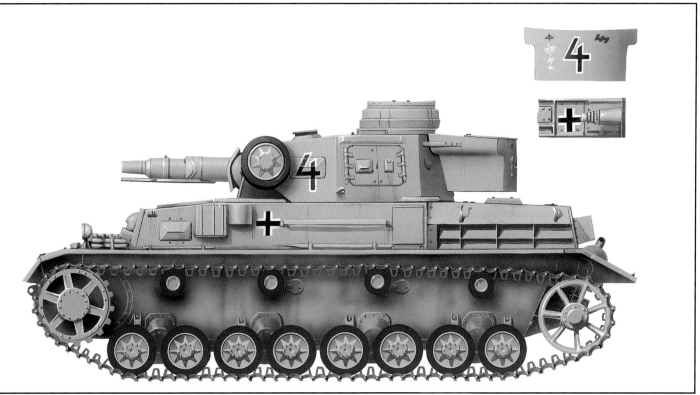

Pz.Kpfw.IV Ausf.F1, Pz.Rgt.8, 15.Panzer-Division, near Tobruk, November 1941

A Pz.Kpfw.IV Ausf.F1 of 4.Kompanie/Pz.Rgt.8. The tactical number '4' is painted in black with a white outline on each side of the turret and also on the rear of the turret stowage bin. A national cross appears on each side of the hull in black with a white outline which has also been repeated on the lower right side of the rear plate beside the idler mount. The Divisional emblem, a red triangle with a vertical line through it, is painted on the front plate and again on the upper left corner of the stowage bin, along with the red Panzer-Regiment 8 'Wolfsangel' insignia on the upper right side. A white DAK palm emblem has been painted on the front plate next to the ball mount machine gun as well as below the Divisional emblem on the stowage bin. The vehicle has a fairly new uniform coat of sand yellow (RAL 8000) paint over the dark gray (RAL 7021) base.

StuG.III Ausf.C/D, Sonderverband z.b.V.288, 90.leichte Afrika-Division, Bir Hacheim, May 1942

These vehicles were painted in brown (RAL 8020) and khaki gray (RAL 7008) when they arrived in Africa in early 1942. A thin black outline national cross, in turn outlined in white, was painted on each side and on the smoke candle housing on the rear of the vehicle. The unit's emblem, a green wreath encircling a palm tree and rising sun with a small swastika at the bottom, was painted on the front plate on the right side of the main gun.

7.62cm F.K.296(r) auf Zgkw. 5t, Pz.Jg.Abt.605, Tel el Eisa, July 1942

The vehicle has a badly worn coat of sand yellow (RAL 8000) paint applied over the dark gray (RAL 7021) base. Markings are restricted to a white single digit tactical number painted on each side plus the standard Wehrmacht vehicle license plate on the front and a small white elephant on the left rear of the fighting compartment. A white air recognition band was also painted across the top of the engine compartment.

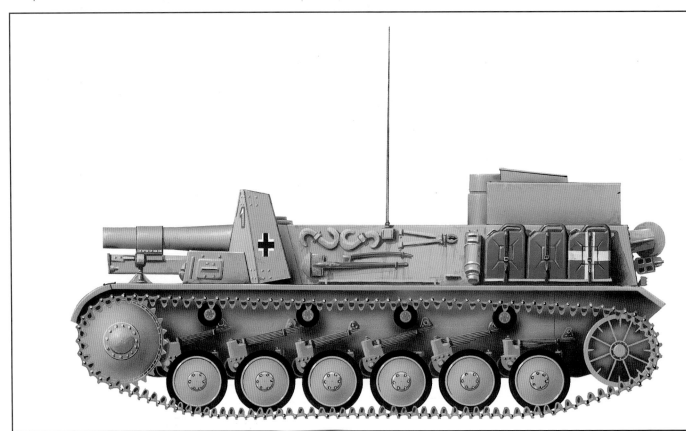

15cm s.I.G.33 B Sfl., s.I.G.Kp.(mot.S) 707 or 708, Libya, 1942

This vehicle has received a new coat of sand yellow (RAL 8000) paint over the original dark gray (RAL 7021) base. Markings seem to have varied on each gun. Here they are limited to a black national cross with a white outline and a single digit tactical number '1' painted in white leaving a thin border of the original dark gray paint around it.

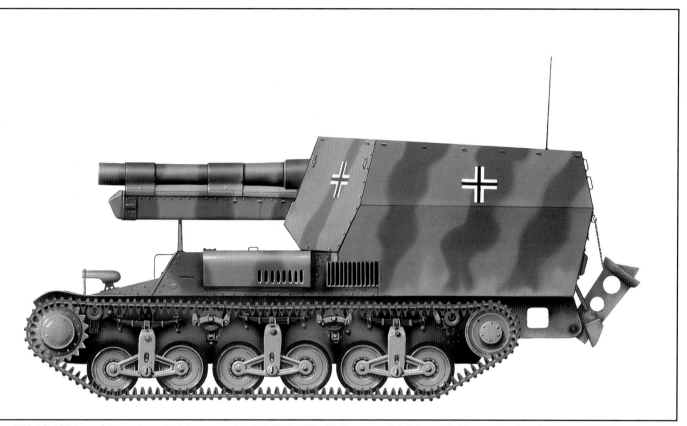

5cm s.F.H.13 (Sfl.) auf Lorraine-Schlepper, Pz.Art.Rgt.155, 21.Panzer-Division, El Alamein, September 1942

This vehicle is finished with a coat of Afrika braun (RAL 8020) camouflaged with dark gray (RAL 7021) stripes. National crosses, painted in black with a white outline, were applied to both the side and front plates of the fighting compartment and on the rear access door. On the left side of the rear plate the white tactical signs for 21.Panzer-Division and a towed artillery company were painted with the DAK palm on the right. These were also repeated on the curved part of the front mudguards.

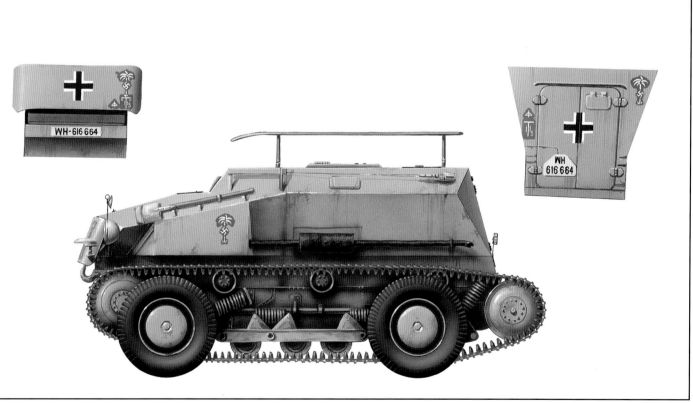

d.Kfz.254 m.gep.Beob.Kw (Saurer RK7), Pz.Art.Rgt.33, 15.Panzer-Division, El Alamein, October 1942

Vehicle markings consist of a black national cross with a white outline painted in the middle of the front plate and centered on the rear access doors. The DAK palm emblem, 15.Panzer-Division emblem and the tactical sign for 5.Batterie of a towed artillery Abteilung have been painted in white on the front. These have been repeated on the rear and the DAK palm also appears on the left side of the engine compartment. Standard Wehrmacht license plates - WH-616664 - have been applied to the front and rear. The markings were painted on the dark gray (RAL 7021) base and then carefully painted around with the sand yellow (RAL 8000) camouflage color.

Sd.Kfz.251/10 Ausf.B, unit unknown, El Alamein, November 1942
This platoon commander's vehicle displays a very worn coat of sand yellow (RAL 8000) paint applied over the dark gray (RAL 7021) base
Visible markings include a newly painted white outline national cross and the standard vehicle license. The faint remains of a white tactica
number '13' can also be seen behind the national cross.

4.7cm PaK(t) auf Pz.Kpfw.I Ausf.B, Pz.Jg.Abt.605, El Alamein, November 1942
This Panzerjäger IB has received a coat of sand yellow (RAL 8000) or brown (RAL 8020) applied over the dark gray (RAL 7021) base colc
The dark area around the top of the gun shield is where the original paint was left intact when the vehicle was painted with canvas cover le
in place. There are no apparent markings although it is possible a white outline national cross may be applied on the rear plate.

Panzerjäger 38(t) fur 7.62cm PaK36(r), Marder III, unknown Pz.Jg.Abt., El Alamein, November 1942
Most vehicles of this type were painted with a coat of sand yellow (RAL 8000) or brown (RAL 8020) over the dark gray (RAL 7021) base. Markings consist of a black national cross with white outline on each side and probably the rear.

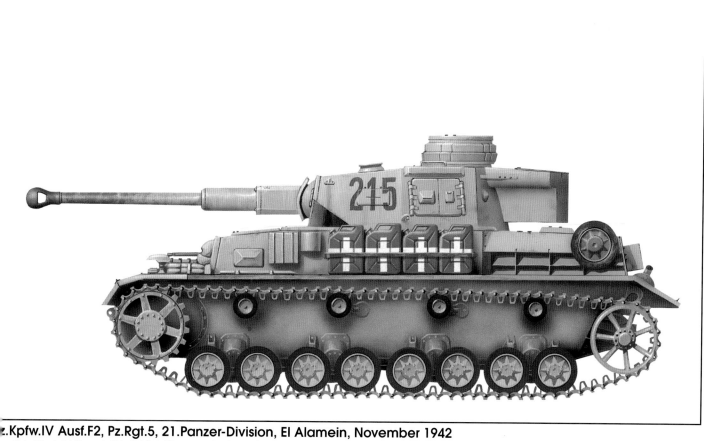

Pz.Kpfw.IV Ausf.F2, Pz.Rgt.5, 21.Panzer-Division, El Alamein, November 1942
This Mark IV 'Special' is finished in a coat of sand yellow (RAL 8000) applied over the dark gray (RAL 7021) base. The tactical number '215' has been painted on the turret in red.

Pz.Kpfw.IV Ausf.G, Pz.Rgt.5, 21.Panzer-Division, Gabes, April 1943
This Pz.Kpfw.IV Ausf.G is probably finished in brown (RAL 8020) painted over the dark gray (RAL 7021) base. An attempt has been made to camouflage the distinctive long barrel 7.5cm gun by applying the brown paint in stripes. A tactical number '852' is painted in red on the side of the turret, an unusual style. The black national crosses have had the white outline painted over with the brown paint.

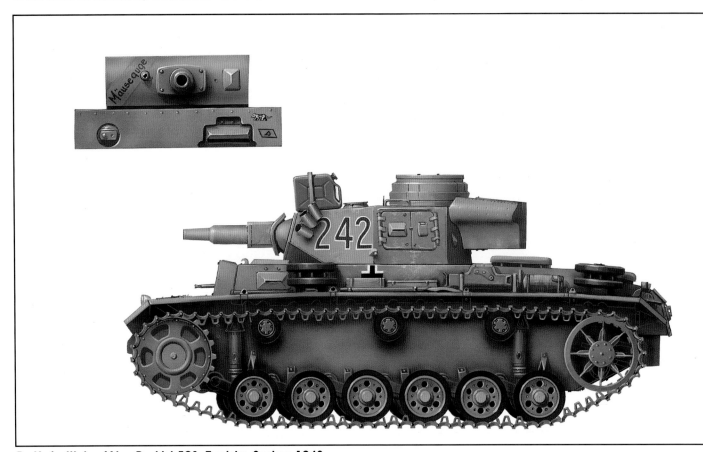

Pz.Kpfw.III Ausf.N, s.Pz.Abt.501, Tunisia, Spring 1943
One of 25 Pz.Kpfw.III Ausf.N support vehicles with this heavy Tiger tank battalion, it is finished in brown (RAL 8020) that has been applied over the dark gray (RAL 7021) base. A tactical number '242' has been painted on the side of the turret in red with a white outline. The stalking tiger emblem of this unit is displayed in black and yellow above a red rhombus with the script letter 's' inside of it on the top right corner of the spaced armor plate on the front of the vehicle, and was probably repeated on the rear plate as well. A black national cross with a white outline appeared on both sides and on the rear plate in the standard location. The crew has painted the name 'Mäuseauge' in red letters on an olive green bar across the mantlet. Literally translated it means 'mice eyes'.

One of the more unique vehicles of the Afrika Korps encountered by the British is this schwere Panzerspähwagen Sd.Kfz.231 mounting a 5cm PaK 38 anti-tank gun. The armored car's normal turret was probably damaged beyond repair creating the opportunity for an ingenious field modification.

British troops take cover beside an abandoned schwere Panzerspähwagen (Fu) Sd.Kfz.232 bearing the name 'Gerd v. Hohendorff' in white on a patch of the original dark gray color paint. Other markings include the vehicle registration number on the front, a white outline black national cross on the side and a DAK palm emblem on the spaced armor plate. The vehicle has had a fairly uniform coat of sand yellow camouflage paint applied over the dark gray. It has probably been abandoned for some time as the 2cm KwK 30 main armament has been removed.

Dense, black smoke pours out of this destroyed Pz.Kpfw.III making an exact identification impossible. Judging from the absence of ash build up from the burnt rubber tires, it seems likely that this vehicle was previously destroyed and the photograph has been staged.

This Pz.Kpfw.III Ausf.J burns as a result of being hit by British guns. Note the build up of ash around the burnt rubber tires. The force of the explosion has dislodged the recoil housing and allowed the 5cm KwK L/42 gun to retract into the turret.

Australian or New Zealand troops pose with a knocked out Pz.Kpfw.III Ausf.J from 3.Kompanie/Pz.Rgt.8. An internal explosion has broken the weld along the side of the superstructure and pushed out the side plate. The vehicle is finished with sand yellow paint applied over the dark gray base and has a red tactical number '3' painted on the turret.

One of the 76 Pz.Kpfw.III Ausf.L with the 5cm KwK L/60 gun, shipped to North Africa in July and August 1942. They were to become known to the British as 'Mark III Specials' because of their long gun. This one, like many others, is missing the 20mm spaced armor plate on the mantlet. Other changes in the Ausf.L included the addition of a 20mm spaced armor plate on the front of the hull, deletion of the loader's vision flap in the mantlet and both turret side view ports. It is finished in a uniform coat of sand yellow paint over the dark gray base and displays an oversized national cross on the front and red with white outline tactical numbers on the turret sides and stowage bin. The tactical number indicates it is from 7.Kompanie/Pz.Rgt.5.

A Pz.Kpfw.III Ausf.J mounting the [c]cm KwK L/42 gun captured at El [A]lamein. It has been refitted with the [2]0mm spaced armor plates on the front [o]f the hull and turret that were normally [fi]tted on the Ausf.L. The tactical [n]umber '722' indicates it is also from [2].Kompanie/Pz.Rgt.5 but notice how [d]ifferent the number style is from the [p]revious photo. The contrast between [th]e color of the numbers and the [v]ehicle suggest they are probably [p]ainted in black.

Two photos of the 4.7cm PaK (t) auf. Pz.Kpfw.I Ausf.B knocked out by British forces in North Africa. Twenty-seven of these vehicles arrived in Tripoli [w]ith Pz.Jg.Abt.605 in March 1941 and saw service throughout the North African campaign to the capitulation in May 1943. It was armed with the Skoda [4]7mm Kanon KPUV.vz38 Model A5 anti-tank gun which was the most potent anti-tank weapon available in the German arsenal when the first Panzerjäger [were produced in 1940. All of them were painted with sand yellow camouflage over their original dark gray base.

Two of the three Panzerjäger I captured by [th]e British at the second battle of El Alamein in [N]ovember 1942. Both are painted with sand [y]ellow over the dark gray base which has been [a]pplied while the canvas covers were still in [pl]ace leaving a strip of the base color around the [to]p of the gun shield. No markings are evident [e]xcept for the 5 white kill rings around the barrel [o]f the nearest vehicle. The Panzerjäger I behind [it] was sent back to England for evaluation and its [e]ventual fate is unknown. One of the others was [s]hipped to Aberdeen Proving Grounds in the [U]nited States. It was sent back to Germany in [1]981 where it currently is on display at the WTS [m]useum in Koblenz.

A leichte Panzerspähwagen Sd.Kfz.221 fitted with a 2.8cm sPzB41 anti-tank gun mounted in a modified turret. They replaced the MG34 armed versions starting in 1942 and saw service with the Aufklärungs Abteilungen of the light Panzer and motorized infantry divisions.

The DAK received 9 Pz.Kpfw.IV Ausf.F2 in May 1942. They were armed with the 7.5cm KwK40 L/43, the most powerful tank gun on either side until the arrival of the Tiger I in late 1942. Here, the crew have supplemented the frontal armor by adding sand bags on the hull. So desperate was the need for replacements at the front, they were initially sent into action without having any markings applied.

One of the identifying features of the Pz.Kpfw.IV Ausf.F2 is the globular muzzle brake as seen here. This vehicle has been painted with sand yellow over the original dark gray base. It has a red tactical number '4' painted on the turret indicating it is from 4 Kompanie/Pz.Rgt.8 and a white outlined black national cross painted on the side of the hull. The object projecting forward from the cupola is an early style of anti-aircraft machine gun mount which the arms of the folded bipod were attached to.

A 15cm s.I.G.33 B Sfl. from s.I.G.Kp.(mot.S) 707 or 708 that has been destroyed by an anti-tank round that has set off the ammunition stored in the back of the vehicle. Twelve of these self-propelled guns were sent to Libya, six in February 1942 and the remainder in April. The weight of the gun overloaded the chassis and they suffered from many automotive problems during their short combat history. After the battle of El Alamein, the British reported capturing six in various states of repair. German reports indicate that all were lost by December 2, 1942.

This Pz.Kpfw.II Ausf.A-C lies abandoned somewhere in the Western Desert. A white DAK palm emblem and the emblem of 21.Panzer-Division are painted on the front plate. It has been fitted with the later cupola and 15mm additional armor plates bolted to the mantlet.

A late model leichte Panzerspähwagen (2cm) Sd.Kfz.222 lies in a British vehicle dump after the retreat from El Alamein. It is finished with a coat of sand yellow paint applied over the dark gray base color and displays a white outlined black national cross on each side and on the rear of the armored cowling protecting the radiator. The ever present jerry can racks have been mounted on the front and rear mudguards.

British soldiers inspect another Sd.Kfz.222 that looks relatively intac however note the penetration hole in the front plate next to the storage bo It is similarly marked to the other vehicle but the remnants of a tactica marking appear on the left side engine compartment access door. Th vehicle registration number - WH 607858 - is painted on the front and rea and a faint 15.Panzer-Division emblem can be seen on the left mudguar between the Notek light base and headlight.

This Pz.Kpfw.III Ausf.L exhibits some damage from anti-tank gun fire the drive sprocket and rear idler. It is missing the 20mm spaced armor pla in front of the mantlet that was commonly seen on the earlier vehicles of th type. Note as well the deletion of the hull side escape hatch and turret visio ports. Several spare track pins can be seen projecting out of the armore ventilation housing located on the side of the engine deck.

An interesting series of photos of a Pz.Kpfw.III Ausf.L taken while it was abandoned in the open desert and again, after it had been towed back to a vehicle dump in the rear area. The early MG34 anti-aircraft mount bolted to the cupola is clearly visible as well as the deletion of the loader's visor in the mantlet. However, it still retains the side escape hatch. Note the piles of ammunition removed from the vehicle laying on the ground - there are no less than 97 rounds. A normal load was 92 rounds for the Pz.Kpfw.III Ausf.L.

A closeup of the 20mm spaced armor plate and its attachment brackets on a Pz.Kpfw.III Ausf.J or Ausf.L. This photo also provides a good view of the attachment bracket for the vehicle horn. Note the expended projectile on the glacis below the muzzle of the MG34.

A Pz.Kpfw.III Ausf.L from 3.Kompanie/Pz.Rgt.8 knocked out during the fighting around Tobruk. The sign laying on the ground beside the tank says 'ACROMA 72 MILES'.

This early Pz.Kpfw.III Ausf.G is one of the original vehicles shipped to North Africa with Pz.Rgt.5 in March 1941. The tactical number '525' can still be seen on the turret stowage bin and would also appear on the sides of the turret. Unusually, two white outline black national crosses have been painted on the left side along with the white emblem of 21.Panzer-Division.

This Pz.Kpfw.IV Ausf.F2 appears to have become bogged down in soft sand which has immobilized it. Note the antenna deflector mounted under the gun, which was peculiar to the Ausf.F2. The crew has tried to improve the protection of their vehicle with additional tracks links fastened to the front of the hull and superstructure including spare wheels that look as though they might have come from a British Grant tank.

The crew of this Pz.Kpfw.IV Ausf.F2 has gone to great lengths to camouflage their tank from the enemy. A single digit tactical number, a black or red '8', has been painted on the side of the turret and, unusually, on the side of the stowage bin. Several sets of spare roadwheels are carried on this side of the vehicle including a set that is missing the rubber tyres.

A destroyed Pz.Kpfw.IV Ausf.F2 is removed from the battlefield by British troops on a German 22/23 ton tank transporter trailer, Sd.Ah.116. A two digit tactical number '12' can be seen on the turret, probably in red with a white outline. An internal explosion has blown off the whole side of the superstructure which has also peeled off the sheet metal mudguard on this side. Note the three different tire tread patterns on the wheels of the trailer.

Another destroyed Pz.Kpfw.IV Ausf.F2 and two Pz.Kpfw.II one of which can be identified as an Ausf.L, from Pz.Rgt.5. Th tactical number '114' is red with a white outline and there is black and white national cross on the side of the hull. Thes vehicles were knocked out during the battle at El Alamein.

A 15cm s.F.H.13 (Sfl.) auf Lorraine-Schlepper from Pz.Art.Rgt.155, 21.Panzer-Division, destroyed at El Alamein in September 1942. Twenty-three of these self-propelled howitzers were shipped to North Africa in July and August 1942, ten to Pz.Art.Rgt.155 and thirteen to Pz.Art.Rgt.33 of 15.Panzer-Division. All were reported to have been destroyed by December 2, 1942.

A series of photos of two of the S.F.H.13 (Sfl.) that were captured intact during the battle at El Alamein. They are finished in a pattern of wavy sa yellow lines applied over the dark gray base. One of them is prominently marked with black and white national crosses on the front, sides and rear alo with a white tactical sign for a towed artillery company and the 21.Panzer-Division emblem. The latter also appear on the left mudguard with a white DA palm emblem painted on the right mudguard. The two unmarked vehicles are probably from Pz.Art.Rgt.33 of 15.Panzer-Division.

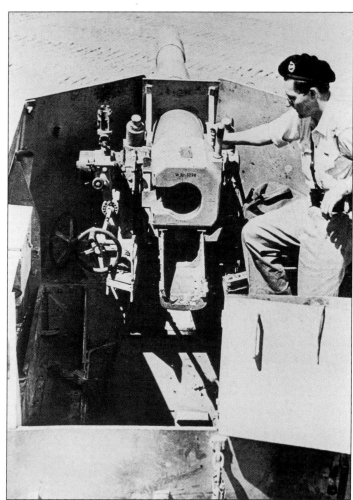

This 7.62cm F.K.296(r) auf Zgkw. 5t of Pz.Jg.Abt.605 was captured by the British at Tel el Eisa, near El Alamein in July 1942. Nine of these vehicles were shipped to North Africa, arriving in January and February 1942. In early March, they were assigned to 90.leichte Division. Gradually, one after another, they were all destroyed or lost by the end of November 1942. The British nicknamed these vehicles 'Diana'.

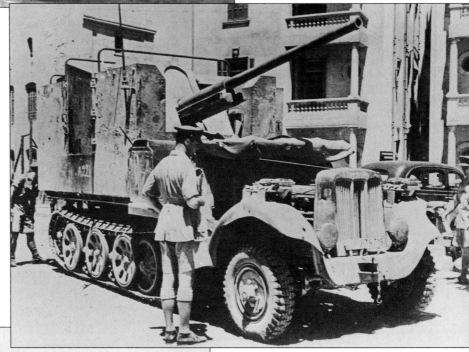

One of the rarer vehicles used by the DAK is the Sd.Kfz.254 m.gep.Beob.Kw (Saurer RK7) from Pz.Art.Rgt.33, 15.Panzer-Division, captured at El Alamein in October 1942. Only 128 of these vehicles were built by the Austrian firm of Saurer. It is not known how many served in North Africa, but there are only photographs of two known vehicles that did. This one was sent to England for evaluation and the other to Aberdeen Proving Grounds in the United States. The Aberdeen vehicle was returned to Germany in the 1970's and is currently awaiting restoration.

Two photos of the same Sd.Kfz.251/10 Ausf.B of an unknown unit abandoned at El Alamein in November 1942. This platoon commander's vehicle was armed with the obsolete 3.7cm PaK 35/36 to provide some infantry support fire. Markings include a white outline national cross on the sides with a faint white tactical number '13' painted beside it and the standard Wehrmacht vehicle registration number on the front. In the second photo, the gun has been removed.

A Pz.Kpfw.IV Ausf.F2 from Pz.Rgt.5, 21.Panzer-Division abandoned at El Alamein in November 1942. This Mark IV 'Special' is finished in a coat of sand llow applied over the dark gray base. The tactical number '215' has been painted on the turret in red. Additional spare track links and sand bags have en added to the glacis in an effort to increase the protection. The white crosses on the jerry cans indicate they were used for carrying water.

One of three StuG.III Ausf.C/D originally from Sonderverband z.b.V.288 attached to 90.leichte Afrika-Division. These vehicles were painted in Afrika braun and khaki gray when they arrived in North Africa in early 1942. A thin black outline national cross, in turn outlined in white, was painted on each side and on the smoke candle housing on the rear of the vehicle. The unit's emblem, a green wreath encircling a palm tree and rising sun with a small swastika at the base, was painted on the front plate on the right side of the main gun. On October 31, 1942 the unit was redesignated Panzer-Grenadier Regiment (mot) Afrika. This one was captured by the British at El Alamein.

A British soldier pose on a knocked c Pz.Kpfw.IV Ausf.F2. Fire ha consumed some of th rubber from the roadwhee and burned off the pa from the side of the tar Part of the tactical numbe an '8', is still visible on t side of the turret.

This Panzerjäger 38(t) fur 7.62cm PaK36(r) Marder III was dug into a defensive position and overrun by the British during the battle at El Alamein in November 1942. Sixty-six Marder III were shipped to North Africa from July to November 1942 where they were assigned to Pz.Jg.Abt.33 of 15.Panzer-Division and Pz.Jg.Abt.39 of 21.Panzer-Division. Most were painted with a coat of sand yellow or brown over the dark gray base. In the background is a Pz.Kpfw.III Ausf.J with the 5cm KwK39 L/60 gun. This Marder III is probably from Pz.Jg.Abt.39.

Two photos of a Marder III disabled by a mine blast that has blown off one of the roadwheels and broken the track. These vehicles were armed with captured Russian 76.2mm M1936 field gun, designated FK296 by the Germans, the same gun that was installed on the 'Diana'. It was redesigned and chambered to take the German PaK 40 ammunition. Markings are limited to a black and white national cross painted on the sides and on the smoke candle cover on the rear of the vehicle.

Another Marder III from the same unit that has suffered the same fate along the same road.

This Marder III has been collected from the battlefield and taken to a British vehicle dump probably for shipment back to England for evaluation. There appears to be little in the way of damage and even the paint is in good condition.

This apparently undamaged Marder III is towing an ammunition trailer. The Marder III was equipped to carry only 30 rounds of ammunition.

ive photos of Marder III knocked out in Libya and Tunisia in late 1942 and early 1943.

A BMW R12 motorcycle combination from Pz.Rgt.7 of 10.Panzer-Division in Tunisia in December 1942. The Division was transferred to Tunisia from Southern France in November and was immediately committed to battle with XC.Korps during their attempt to widen the Tunis Bridgehead. The German soldier repairing the flat tire seems to have attracted a large crowd of curious citizens.

A Pz.Kpfw.III Ausf.L from Pz.Rgt.7 of 10.Panzer-Division concealed in an olive grove in Tunisia in December 1942. The emblem painted on the right side of the rear hull is a stylized club playing card symbol that appears to be black with a white outline. Other photos of this unit's Pz.Kpfw.III shows this marking also painted on the lower side of the turret stowage bin.

A schwere Panzerspähwagen (7.5cm) Sd.Kfz.233 rolls down a street through a Tunisian town in late December 1942. At this late date, the crew are still wearing the tropical pith helmet with their tropical issue uniform. The terrain in Tunisia was quite different than the Libyan desert, with large areas of trees and vegetation providing additional materials to help camouflage the vehicles.

Another s.Pz.Sp.Wg. Sd.Kfz.233 in Tunisia in January 1943. 109 of these vehicles were produced from December 1942 until October 1943 and were armed with the obsolete 7.5cm StuK 37 L/24 gun from the earlier Pz.Kpfw.IV.

The driver of this BMW R75 motorcycle combination scans the horizon through his binoculars for signs of the enemy in Tunisia in December 1942. The emblem painted on the back of the sidecar is that of Fallschirmjäger-regiment 5, a black comet with a tail streaming out behind it. The crew of the 7.5cm PaK 40 anti-tank gun seem to have made a half-hearted effort at camouflaging their gun.

The battered remains of two Pz.Kpfw.II Ausf.F lie beside the road after the battle for Mateur in Tunisia, December 1942.

An 8.8cm FlaK 18 anti-aircraft gun of a Luftwaffe Flak-Regiment fires at ground targets near Tebourba in January 1943. The gun is carried on the newer Sd.Ah.202 trailer, equipped with four sets of dual tired wheels, which is waiting close by in case the gun needs to be moved in a hurry. The crew seem to all be wearing the Luftwaffe tropical uniform with the large patch pocket on the left leg of the trousers. The crewman in the foreground has the Flakartilleriepersonal specialist badge on his left sleeve which was awarded after nine months service.

This Sd.Kfz.7 half-track prime mover has been loaded to capacity with wooden crates, trunks and duffel bags containing the troops personal gear. As the Germans retreated farther into Tunisia, it became necessary to carry everything of value with them. This photo was taken in February 1943.

An NSU HK100 Kettenkraftrad Kfz.2 captured by the British in Tunisia. The Kettenkrad, as it was called, could carry a crew of three including the operator. Two men sat behind the driver facing the rear with their rifles mounted in the special racks on the back. This one displays the DAK palm emblem stenciled on the side.

Another Kettenkrad destroyed when small arms fire ignited the fuel from its gas tanks causing the vehicle to burn. It is towing the standard trailer built especially for use with the Kettenkrad. The remains of a Divisional Services tactical marking, a rectangle with an 'X' inside, can be seen on the side of the engine compartment.

A Pz.Kpfw.III Ausf.N, probably from s.Pz.Abt.501, destroyed in Tunisia in 1943. Note the two impact points on the side of the hull. Twenty-five Pz.Kpfw.III Ausf.N were shipped to North Africa with this Tiger I battalion as fire support vehicles.

One of several U.S. Army M3 half-tracks captured intact by the Germans at Kasserine Pass in February 1943 and put to use. The prominent American star has been painted over and a white outline national cross added to identify it. It is an early production M3 without the mine rack on the side.

An 8.8cm FlaK 36/37 anti-aircraft gun destroyed by the British in Tunisia. Externally, it was identical to the FlaK 18 except for the barrel of the gun and the trailer, although it was not uncommon to see a FlaK 18 barrel on a FlaK 36/37 carriage.

This damaged Pz.Kpfw.III Ausf.J has been fitted with the additional 20mm spaced armor plate on the front of the hull but not on the turret. The 5cm kwK gun barrel is missing leaving only the armored housing which gives it the appearance of having the short 7.5cm gun. Two of the three digits in the tactical number are visible, '23', the last digit being obscured by the spare track section hanging from the turret.

U.S. Army soldiers pose with an early Pz.Kpfw.IV Ausf.G. Note the vision ports on the side of the turret and the loader's vision port beside the mantlet have been deleted, however, it still retains the globular muzzle brake associated with the Ausf.F2. There have been several additional brackets welded onto the turret roof and front to hang spare track sections from and brackets on the hull to hold spare roadwheels.

A derelict Sd.Kfz.11 half-track prime mover abandoned in the desert. These vehicles were mainly used to tow the 10.5cm leFH 18 howitzer in addition to other types of anti-tank and field artillery. The only visible marking is the Wehrmacht registration number painted on the rear.

Three U.S. Army soldiers inspect an abandoned Sd.Kfz.8 12 ton half-track prime mover. The vehicle has caught fire which has burned off the rubber from the roadwheels along with most of the paint as well.

This schwere Panzerspähwagen (7.5cm) Sd.Kfz.233 was captured in Tunisia. It is painted with sand yellow over the original dark gray base. The only marking displayed is the vehicle registration number, WH - 237 778, painted in black on a white background.

A captured schwere Panzerspähwagen Sd.Kfz.231 is examined by British war correspondents. The object attached to the side of the turret is a smoke discharger. The vehicle is painted with a mottled sand yellow camouflage scheme applied over the dark gray base. Other than the vehicle registration number, the only other marking is a number '8' painted on a small square patch of the dark gray base color, on the top right corner of the spaced armor plate.

Two British sappers race away from a Pz.Kpfw.III Ausf.L, knocked out in the Medenine area in March 1943, after placing a satchel charge in the open turret to blow it up. The large white tactical number '632' indicates the vehicle is probably from Pz.Rgt.5. Like most Pz.Kpfw.III Ausf.L seen in North Africa, it is missing the 20mm spaced armor plate on the front of the turret.

A Pz.Kpfw.II Ausf.A-C that has been consumed by fire. The rubber off the last three roadwheels and the return rollers has been burned off as well as the paint on the side of the hull and turret. A white outline national cross and part of the first tactical number are still visible on the turret. The last Pz.Kpfw.II were delivered to the Wehrmacht in December 1942.

Two schwerer Panzerspähwagen (7.5cm) Sd.Kfz.233 in Tunisia in March 1943. Both vehicles carry additional gear stowed on the outside and jerry cans for water. The nearest one is marked only with the standard Wehrmacht registration plates on the rear and a black and white national cross on the side of the hull.

A Pz.Kpfw.III Ausf.N of the headquarters Company of Pz.Abt.501. There were five of these tanks in the company with red and white outline tactical numbers '03' to '07'. This one appears to be either '03' or '05'. Seven hundred Pz.Kpfw.III Ausf.N were produced from June 1942 to August 1943, mostly on the Ausf.L chassis, like this one.

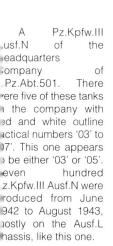

A mixed column of German and American half-tracks and Pz.Kpfw.III Ausf.N on the move after Operation 'Eilbote I' around March, 1943. The Sd.Kfz.251/1 Ausf.C in the foreground is a rare riveted hull vehicle and has the tactical sign for 10.Panzer-Division, a 'Y' with three vertical bars beside it, painted on a dark gray patch of the original color on the front plate.

An Sd.Kfz.7 half-track prime mover towing a 15cm sFH 1 howitzer through the Tunisian desert in March 1943. Th German censor has scratched out the vehicles registratio number plates painted on each side of the front bumper.

This Sd.Kfz.251/1 Ausf.C appears to have been fitted with a 5cm PaK 38 anti-tank gun by the field workshop. The MG34 gun shield usually positione on the front, has been relocated to the rear. A DAK palm emblem and a thin black and white national cross are painted on the rear doors. The vehicle rather battered looking, missing the doors to the storage lockers on the side and the front mudguard.

A Pz.Kpfw.IV Ausf.G of Pz.Rgt.5 knocked out during the battle at Gabes in April 1943. The unusual style tactical numbers have been painted on the turret in red and a plain black national cross is visible just above the jack. The vehicle is likely painted with Afrika braun over the dark gray base color. An attempt to camouflage the long gun has been made by applying the braun paint in stripes on the barrel.

This Pz.Kpfw.III Ausf.L of Pz.Rgt.7, 10.Panzer-Division was knocked by the British in the Kasserine area in February 1943. The tactical number '1' is painted in a black outline on the turret along with two smaller numbers, '15' not visible in this photograph, below it. Note as well the missing 20mm spaced armor plate on the mantlet.

A Pz.Kpfw.IV Ausf.G and a Pz.Kpfw.III Ausf.L in Tunisia. The 'Wolfsangel' emblem of Pz.Rgt.8 can be seen to the right of the driver's visor. The additional track links and sand bags apparently did not provide much protection for this vehicle.

A Pz.Kpfw.II Ausf.F captured by the U.S. Army in Tunisia. The new owners have painted a white American star, probably on a blue circle, on the turret while leaving the German white outline national cross intact on the storage bin. Another unknown marking has been added behind it. The vehicle displays a very worn coat of sand yellow or Afrika braun over the dark gray base. Otherwise, it is in excellent condition.

Another Pz.Kpfw.II Ausf.F put to work by the U.S. Army in Tunisia after the German surrender. An American star and the name 'SNAFU' have been painted in white on the turret along with a dark band, possibly red in color. A command pennant is attached to the left mudguard bearing the silver oakleaf insignia of a Lt. Colonel while another pennant attached to the right mudguard has an illegible inscription painted on it.

A Pz.Kpfw.IV Ausf.G destroyed by American forces in April 1943. It is a late production vehicle that is equipped with smoke discharger brackets on the turret sides similar to those on the Pz.Kpfw.III Ausf.M and Ausf.N and the new Tiger I's of s.Pz.Abt.501. White outline black national crosses are the only visible markings.

68

This Pz.Kpfw.III Ausf.N was one of the support vehicles sent to Tunisia with s.Pz.Abt.501 and displays the stalking Tiger unit emblem and the tactical sign of a schwere-Panzer-Abteilung, a rhombus with a script 'S' inside, on the front plate to the right of the driver's visor. The tactical number '242' is painted on the turret with red numbers outlined in white. Of particular interest is the nickname 'Mauseauge', literally meaning 'mice eyes', painted in red letters on an olive green band across the mantlet. The frame on top of the turret was a bracket for holding several jerry cans in place.

Two Pz.Kpfw.IV Ausf.G along with the remains of two Tigers that were blown up by their crews to prevent capture. The remaining Tigers in 2.Kompanie/s.Pz.Abt.501 were reorganized and renumbered as 8.Kompanie/Pz.Rgt.7 prior to the beginning of Operation 'Ochsenkopf' on February 26, 1943.

A Pz.Kpfw.VI Ausf.E 'Tiger I' of 1.Kompanie/s.Pz.Abt.504 knocked out near Tunis by British forces. The small white rhombus with a '1' beside it can be seen on the front side of the hull along with a white outline black national cross midway down the side. An internal explosion has blown off the commander's cupola and barrel sleeve, pushing it down against the muzzle brake. Note the Feifel air cleaners just visible on the rear of the vehicle.

Probably the best known Tiger I in the world today is this one, captured intact on April 23, 1943 by the British near Medjez-el-Bab, Tunisia and currently undergoing restoration at the RAC Tank Museum in Bovington, England. It belonged to 1.Kompanie/s.Pz.Abt.504 and had a red tactical number '131' painted on the side of the turret. The white rhombus with the company number beside it is clearly visible on the side of the hull. Here it is seen with the deep wading cover for the ball mount machine gun fitted after it was captured. The vehicle in front is an NSU Kettenkraftrad Kfz.2.

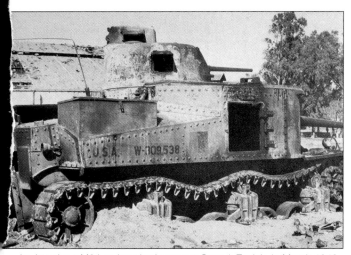

An American M3 Lee knocked out near Sened, Tunisia in March 1943. The serial number is painted in blue on the olive drab base color and a name, possibly 'San Juan', is painted in white just behind the 75mm gun mount. The resulting fire has burned off the paint on the side of the hull and 37mm gun turret, leaving the outline of the yellow or white star painted on the side of the turret faintly visible. The armor of the M3 was no match for the guns of the Pz.Kpfw.IV Ausf. F2 or G and Tiger I.

Another American M3 Lee, fitted with the longer barrel M3 75mm gun, completely burned out near Sened, Tunisia in March 1943. The fire has removed any trace of markings, though the faint outline of the band painted on the turret can be seen. The grisly remains of one of the unfortunate crew members lies on the ground below the open escape hatch.

Bibliography

Balin, George, *Tanks Illustrated No.17, Afrika Korps*, Arms & Armor Press

Bender, R.J. & Law, R.D., *Uniforms, Organization and History of the Afrikakorps*, R. James Bender Publishing

Bradford, George R., *Armor Camouflage & Markings North Africa 1940-1943*, Squadron/Signal Publications

Buffetaut, Yves, *Armes Militaria Magazine No.3, La Guerre Du Desert (I) Tobrouk*

Buffetaut, Yves, *Armes Militaria Magazine No.6, La Guerre Du Desert (II) Bir-Hakeim*

Buffetaut, Yves, *Armes Militaria Magazine No.11, La Guerre Du Desert (III) El Alamein*

Buffetaut, Yves, *Armes Militaria Magazine No.16, La Guerre Du Desert (IV) Operation Supercharge*

Buffetaut, Yves, *Armes Militaria Magazine No.25, Guerre En Tunisie (1) Kasserine*

Buffetaut, Yves, *Armes Militaria Magazine No.28, Guerre En Tunisie (2) La Ligne Mareth*

Chamberlain, P. & Doyle, H., *Encyclopedia of German Tanks of World War Two*, Arms & Armor Press

Chamberlain, P & Gander, T., *WW2 Fact Files, Anti-Aircraft Guns*, Arco Publishing

Chamberlain, P & Gander, T., *WW2 Fact Files, Anti-Tank Weapons*, Arco Publishing

Chamberlain, P & Gander, T., *WW2 Fact Files, Heavy Artillery*, Arco Publishing

Chamberlain, P & Gander, T., *WW2 Fact Files, Light and Medium Field Artillery*, Arco Publishing

Collier, Richard, *The War in the Desert*, Time-Life Books

Culver, Bruce, *Afrika Korps in Action*, Squadron/Signal Publications

Culver, B. & Feist, U., *Schutzenpanzer*, Ryton Publications

Davis, Brian L., *Badges & Insignia of the Third Reich 1933-1945*, Blandford Press

Doyle, H. & Jentz, T., *New Vanguard 19, Stug III Assault Gun 1940-1942*, Reed International Books

Duske, Heiner F., *Nuts & Bolts Vol.7, Panzerjäger I*

Edwards, Roger, *Panzer A Revolution in Warfare, 1939-1945*, Brockhampton Press

Forty, George, *Afrika Korps at War, 1. The Road to Alexandria*, Charles Scribner's Sons

Forty, George, *Afrika Korps at War, 2. The Long Road Back*, Charles Scribner's Sons

Forty, George, *The Armies of Rommel*, Arms & Armor Press

Frank, Reinhard, *German Personnel Cars in Wartime*, Schiffer Publishing Ltd.

Grove, Eric, *Panzerkampfwagen I & II German Light Tanks 1939-45*, Almark Publishing

Gudgin, Peter, *Tanks Illustrated No.28, Panzer Armee Afrika: Tripoli to Tunis*, Arms & Armor Press

Jentz, Thomas L., *Panzer Tracts No.4, Panzerkampfwagen IV*, Darlington Productions Inc.

Jentz, Thomas L., *Rommel's Funnies*, Darlington Productions Inc.

Jentz, Thomas L., *Tank Combat in North Africa, The Opening Rounds*, Schiffer Publishing Ltd.

Jentz, Thomas L., *Germany's Tiger Tanks, Tiger I & II: Combat Tactics*, Schiffer Publishing Ltd.

Jentz, Thomas L., *Panzer Truppen 1*, Schiffer Publishing Ltd.

Jentz, Thomas L., *Panzer Truppen 2*, Schiffer Publishing Ltd.

Jones, Kenneth M., *No.1 Germany North Africa*, Almark Publishing

Macksey, Kenneth, *Rommel: Battles and Campaigns*, Mayflower Books

Macksey, Kenneth, *Afrika Korps*, Ballentine Books

Mesko, Jim, *M3 Lee/Grant in Action*, Squadron/Signal Publications

Milsom, John, *German Military Transport of World War Two*, Arms & Armor Press

Milsom, John, *German Half-Tracked Vehicles of World War 2*, Arms & Armor Press

Munnich, Ralf, *Panzer in Nord-Afrika 1941-1943*, Podzun-Pallas-Verlag

Oliver, Tony, *German Motorcycles World War II*, Almark Publishing

Pz.Kw.1, A re-styled edition of the original British evaluation report.

Quarrie, Bruce, *Panzers in the Desert*, AZTEX Corporation

Quarrie, Bruce, *Men-At-Arms Series 139, German Airborne Troops 1939-45*, Osprey Publishing

Regenberg, Werner, *Captured American & British Tanks under the German Flag*, Schiffer Publishing Ltd.

Rue, John L., *Nuts & Bolts Vol.05, Saurer RK-7 (Sd.Kfz.254)*

Rue, John L., *Sd.Kfz.6 5ton Medium Halftrack*, ISO Publications

Spielberger, W., & Feist, U., *Armor in the Western Desert*, Aero Publishers, Inc.

Spielberger, Walter J., *Sturmgeschütz & Its Variants*, Schiffer Publishing Ltd.

Thomas, Nigel, *Men-At-Arms Series 316, The German Army 1939-45 (2) North Africa & Balkans*, Reed Consumer Books Ltd.

Zaloga, Steven J., *U.S. Half-Tracks in Combat*, Concord Publications Co.